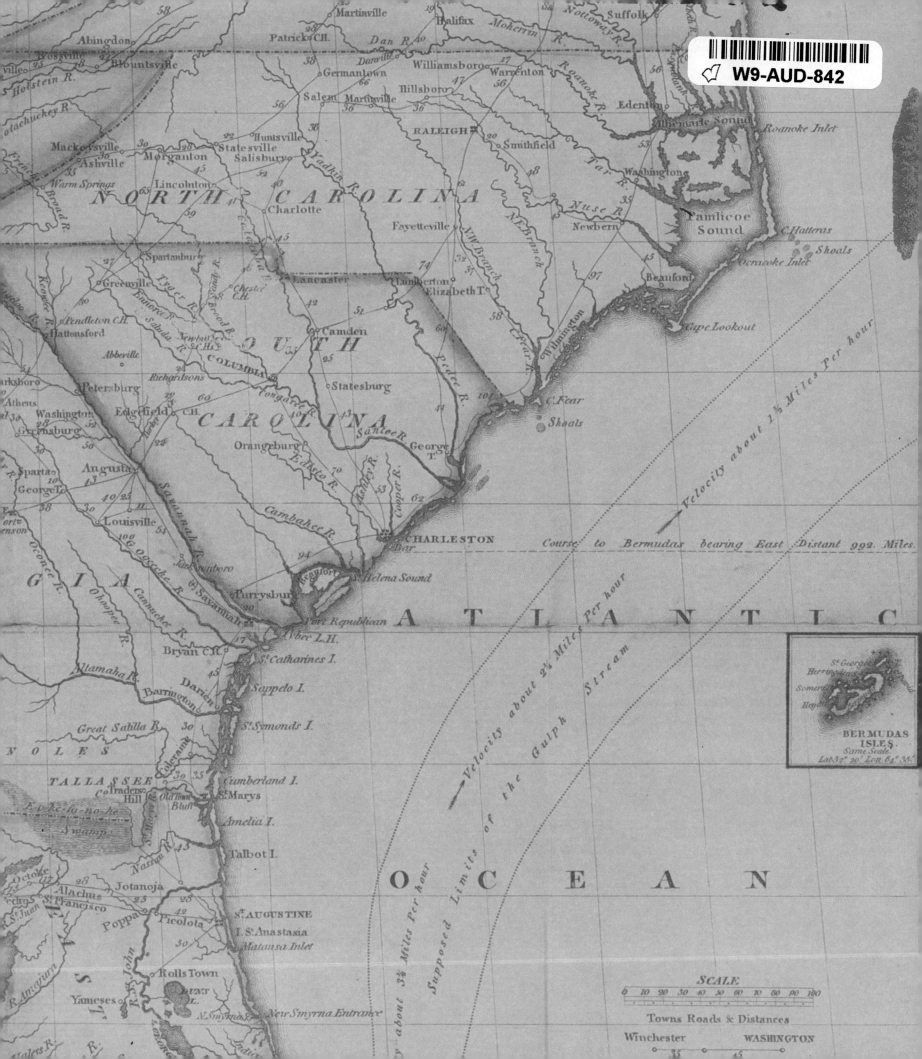

Carolina Nature

A photographer's view of the natural world in the Carolinas

Eric Horan

Carolina Nature

A photographer's view of the natural world in the Carolinas

by

E r i c   H o r a n

Publisher: Southern Light Photographic/ www.southernlight.biz

Printing & Color Separations: Four Colour Imports, Inc.

Printed in China by Everbest, Rep. Four Colour Imports Inc.

Photography: Eric Horan

Professional affiliations: ASMP, NANPA

Introduction: Eric Horan

Forward: Sheila & Dave Metcalf

Graphic Design: Doug Gardner, Eric Horan

Editor: Jan Horan, Lila Meeks

Biological Identification: Bruce Lamplight, Eric Horan

Photo of Eric Horan: Jan Horan

Photo of Boatladderman: Robin Hill

Library of Congress Control Number: 2003094003

ISBN Number: 0-9713715-4-7

Text copyright 2003 Eric Horan and
Dave & Sheila Metcalf. Illustrations
Copyright 2003 Eric Horan

All rights reserved, including the right of reproduction in whole or in part in any form

Foreword

With a simple pass through "Carolina Nature" the reader/viewer can only gasp in wonder. Nature's beauty is uncommonly and remarkably visualized and recorded in this outstanding collection focused on the Carolinas yet bearing down still further on the Lowcountry, that fabled tidewater region of South Carolina.

Eric Horan has devoted much of his life to photographing nature's living participants. The photogapher's eye is an inextricable part of his sense, intellect, aesthetic and soul. Here, we share his soul.

-Dr David R. Metcalf

One needs to stand still in order to see light and shadows, to remain silent to hear the music and rhythm of nature, to be sensitive to all creatures - animals and people - in order to capture their feelings, and an artist to put this awareness together.

Eric, since a small child, has displayed such mingling and organization of senses; and he has been facile at getting his images across to others - family, friends, and acquaintances - in one form or another. When he picked up a camera as a teenager and said, "this is what I want to do" we all knew he would study and move forward with enduring dedication and patience. We observed this with no small amount of envy and admiration.

Few people other than artists are faced with interpreting life, they simply live it. By living in society and stepping out, up, down, or aside in order to interpret its essence, an artist performs a delicate, sometimes difficult balancing act. This balancing act can be physical. Eric's working methods have been at times put in the class of extreme sport, like the time he was hoisted to the top of the mast of a large sailboat during a race, hanging on with one hand and shooting pictures of the deck hands with his camera in the other. Fitted with a 20mm lens and hand held at the end of his out-streched arm, his Canon is supposed to capture the heeling boat held tight to the wind, in focus! And it does. Or, in order to capture the picture of the dolphin surfing in the bowwake, he climbed on the outside of the second deck railing of a fifty-foot trawler and leaned over the hitchhiking mammal. Also, his landscapes are often made from the top of his twelve-foot stepladder from inside his thirteen-foot Boston Whaler. The water is not always calm, probably less so than the photographer.

Eric is blessed with the strength of spirit, creative soul, and heart to share his gifts with others. We are grateful.

-Sheila Metcalf

Acknowledgements

I want to thank my mother and stepfather, Sheila and Dave Metcalf, for their steady belief in me and my abilities; my five siblings - Karen, Steve, Stephanie, Cable and Noah who encourage me in their own individual ways; to my wife's kids, Anna & Elliott who think what I do is "cool" and periodically tell me so.

In my profession, I am grateful for many clients that have supported my work but I wish to recognize a few special clients that stand out in marketing, advertising and design, Tommy Baysden, Patty Boysen, and Donna Martin. Not only have they provided me steady work through the years, but also encour aged me to produce a book of my own work.

Fellow photographers I wish to thank include Eric Satterwhite and David Langley both working at the very top of their profession in New York. I am grateful they encouraged me to come back home. A spe cial thanks to my good friend and photographer Robin Hill who braved lowcountry pluff mud to capture the "boatladderman" picture. I am consistently amazed at my good friend Doug Gardner, photogra pher, graphic artist, confidant and way-shower at half my age. This book would not be realized without his help.

I am grateful to many special friends that have encouraged me in different ways. Thanks to Professor Roy Flannagan and Vice Chancellor Lila Meeks for thoughtful comments that appear in this book. Additional thanks go to Lila for putting her red-editing pen to work on my rough drafts; and Glen Kilgore for prodding me to stay the course. Thanks to biologist Bruce Lamplight for making biological corrections and providing me with gate passes into one of my favorite shooting locations. Last but not least, I am forever grateful to my loving wife, companion, business partner, and editor Jan who has always supported me and encouraged me to pursue my passion.

Introduction

In my experience, everybody has to overcome his or her family dynamics to one degree or another. In my family, I was the lost child, the introvert in an outgoing, gregarious family of five siblings. I struggled with self-consciousness and decision-making that surely inhibited my personal growth for years. Instead of looking from the inside out like I saw others do with ease, I was cursed with a nagging introspection, always judging myself harshly and shrinking from new experiences. I worried a lot and was fearful in new situations that my inadequacies would be discovered. My family moved frequently following my father's clothing stores, forcing me to deal with new communities each change of the season, from winters in Florida, to summers in Michigan.

In a college journalism essay I wrote about my childhood. At night, I experienced a dream world that served as a colorful escape from my crippling self-criticism. My dreams were like Hollywood movies in full color with multiple cuts and roving camera angles from all perspectives. Awakening, I would sit up in bed and try to re-create the cinematography in my mind. This carried over into my daily activities. I began to 'see' my world from a variety of different perspectives, imagining aerial views or wondering what a subject or action might look like if viewed from the ground up or passing by it instead of simply looking at eye level.

In photography, studying one's subject, being able to predict what will happen next and pre-visualizing from a variety of different angles is critical to determining the best shot. A split second in the decision determines success or failure. I realized how practiced I was in this technique. I was impressed at how my childhood dreams had infiltrated my photography.

After graduating from college in commercial art and photography, I supported myself running a painting business while shooting sail-boat races for national magazines on the side. I was living on Hilton Head Island and growing more interested in capturing on film the natural beauty of the coastal southeast, less interested in the building trade and booming development that was well underway. I made the decision to make a go at photography full-time and sold my construction business. This income provided me the seed money for my photography business and a temporary move to New York City where I worked as a free-lance assistant to some of the top commercial photographers in the industry. I was warned not to assist too long in the city and encouraged to continue building on the body of work I started after a few months of assisting and sharing my portfolio from the southeast, I was told that I had everything I needed to go it alone and should go back home, get busy and get to work!

In spite of my attraction to stay in the city, I was anxious to return to the beauty and drama of the natural world of the lowcountry. I started my commercial photography business, Eric Horan Photography, Inc., and am grateful for the support I have received to pursue my passion. Carolina Nature reflects that passion and I hope that you, dear reader, enjoy a glimpse into this amazing region of our country.

- Eric Horan

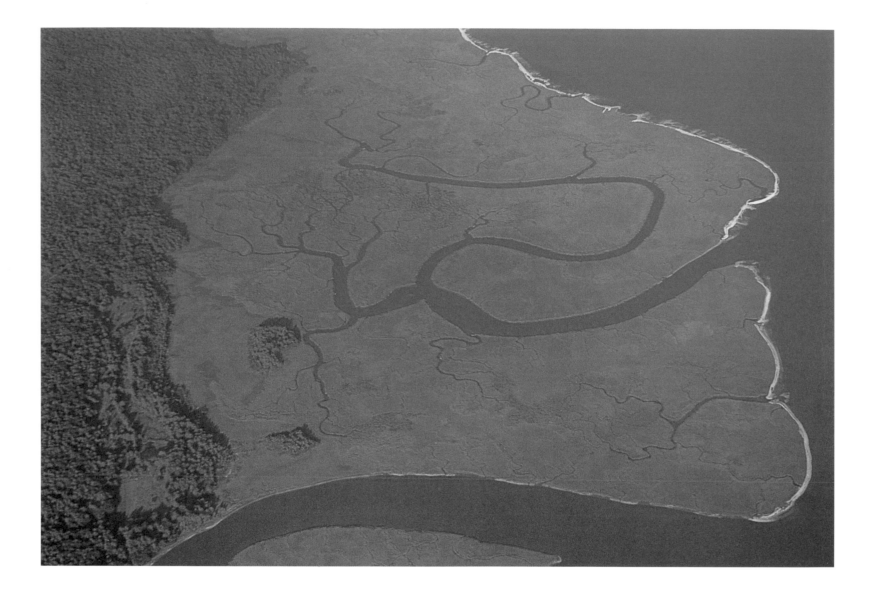

Bull Island, South Carolina

Aerial, Prichards Island, South Carolina

top: Giant Swallow tail / Spanish Moss & Red Bud

Fall colors, Smoky Mountains, North Carolina

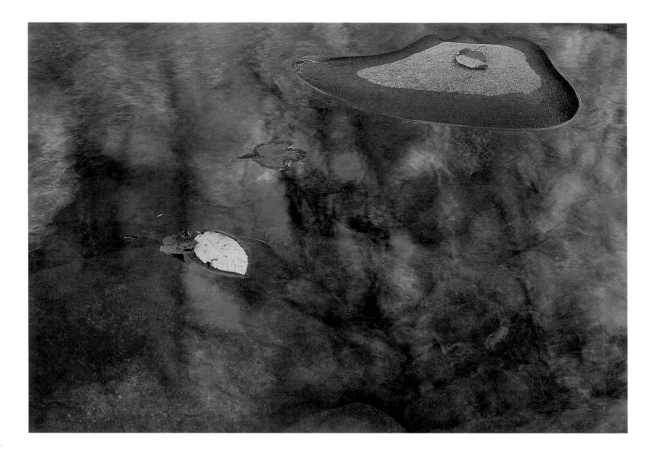

River detail, Boone, North Carolina

Congaree swamp, South Carolina

Ground detail, North Carolina

Cinnamon fern & azalea, South Carolina

Peach blossoms, Aiken, South Carolina

Apple blossoms, Boone, North Carolina

Wood storks nest building, South Carolina

Osprey with catch, Santee, South Carolina

Oystercatcher, Hunting Island, South Carolina

Rose, Beaufort, South Carolina

Yucca, Hilton Head Island South Carolina

Falls at Tremont, North Carolina

Great egret in the rain, Edisto, South Carolina

Summer storm at Pinckney Island, South Carolina

19

Black bear, Lake Mattamuskeet, North Carolina

Falls at Haze creek, South Carolina

River closeup, Lower Whitewater, Falls

Whitetail doe, Sea Pines, South Carolina

Seagull at Sunset, Hilton Head Island, S

Brown pelican portrait, South Carolina

Pre-dawn light, Combahee River, SC

25

Canada geese, Lake Jocassie, SC

Autumn maple, North Carolina

Ring-billed seagull in winter, Edisto Beach, SC

Snowy egret in breeding plummage, Harbor Island, SC

Wet maple leaves, North Carolina

Snow goose on approach, North Carolina

Ice storm, French Broad River, North Carolina

Winter oaks, Lake Mary, Hilton Head Island, SC

Great egret building nest, St. Helena Island, SC

Late spring snow, Smokey Mountains, NC

Cattle egret in rookery, Harbor Island, SC

Tri-colored heron and house, Lands End, SC

Gold finch, Spring Island, SC

Pintail ducks, Lake Mattamuskeet, NC

Wood Duck drake, Spring Island, SC

Boattail grackle, Beaufort, SC

Willets, Capers Island, SC

Boatwake and spartina grass, Hilton Head Island, SC

Tri-colored heron, Port Royal, SC

American alligator in blue lagoon, Kiawah, SC

Great blue heron portrait, Moss Creek, SC

White pelicans migrating, Bull Island, SC

Lowcountry marsh aerial, Beaufort County, SC

Great egret nest building, Pinckney Island, SC

Summer storm, Hilton Head Island, SC

Dolphin following boat, SC

Storm over the ocean, Hunting Island, SC

Osprey catching bass

Osprey in nest, Lake Santee, SC

Bringing home the fish

Summer marsh island, Corn Island, Mackay Creek, SC

Great egret preening, Bulls Island, SC

Small oak at Singleton Beach, Hilton Head Island, SC

Great egret family in nest, Harbor Island, SC

Belted kingfisher on perch, Sea Pines, Hilton Head Island, SC

Dolphin hitchhiking in boatwake, SC

Snowy egret pair nest building, Harbor Island, SC

Dawn on the Harbor River, Harbor Island, SC

Great egret hatchling demanding food, St. Helena Island, SC

Great egret wading for fish, Lemon Island, SC

Snowy egret at the well, St. Helena Island, SC

Great egret and moon, Capers Island, SC

Aerial view of old rice fields, ACE Basin, SC

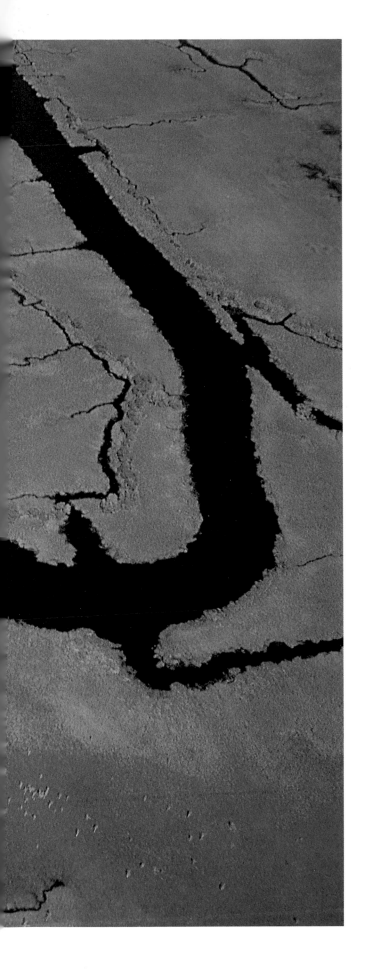

American Oystercatcher and chick, Cooper River, SC

Oystercatcher eggs, Cooper River,SC

Adult Oystercatcher, Bull island, Cooper river, SC

Oystercatcher pair taking flight

Wood storks cooling, Spring Island, SC

Wood storks roosting, Spring Island

Wood stork pair in nest, SC

White ibis in flight, Pinckney Island, SC

Shorebirds in flight, Huntington State Park, SC

Wood stork on perch in fog, Charleston, SC

Arctic tern fishing, Cape Hatteras, NC

Sea oats, Bloody Point, SC

77

Tidal marsh, Bay Point Island, Port Royal Sound, SC

Rainy day saltwater marsh, Edisto beach, SC

Pine tree root in surf, Hunting island, SC

Summer lightning at Pinckney Island, SC

Live oak forest, Spring Island, SC

Whitetail buck, Smoky Mountains, NC

Eye of black crowned night heron, Charleston, SC

Pine trees & cross vine New River, SC

Mixed grasses, Ravenel, SC

Spartina grass at dusk, Labecco, SC

Spartina and clouds, Huntington State Park, SC

Ocean surf at dusk, Coligny Beach, SC

White ibis, Daufuski Island, SC

Wood duck pair, Savannah Wildlife Refuge, SC

Autumn salt marsh, Mackay Creek, SC

Whitetail buck, Boone, North Carolina

Whitetail buck, Sea Pines Plantation, SC

Lurking alligator, Kiawah Island, SC

Watermoccasin, Santee Lake, SC

Haze Creek Falls, SC

Evergreens and fall colors, Smoky Mountains, NC

Autumn forest, Linville Falls, North Carolina

Autumn grasses, Smoky Mtns., NC

First spring leaves near Ashville, North Carolina

River rock and fall reflections, French Broad River

Farm field in fall, Maggie Valley

Willow in the wind, Shenandoah Valley, NC

Wisteria, Summerton, SC

Maple leaves in river, Hot Springs, North Carolina

Blue ridge near Linville Gorge, North Carolina

Cinnamon fern, Myrtle Beach State Park, South Carolina

Azaleas, Callawassie Island, South Carolina

Alley of oaks, Edisto Island, South Carolina

Screech owl, Hilton Head Island, SC

Mink portrait, Bull Creek, South Carolina

Raccoon trot, Pinckney Island, South Carolina

Great blue heron in cypress, Lake Marion, SC

Cumulus clouds and spartina grass, Broad River, SC

Beaver swimming, Hampton, South Carolina

Family of deer, Sea Pines Forest Preserve, SC

Dolphin surfing in wake of boat, offshore, SC

Summer salt marsh, Chechessee River, SC

Wisteria, Whale Branch River, Seabrook, SC

Grackle calling at dusk, Savannah River, South Carolina

Anhinga drying wings, Spring Island, South Carolina

Crepe Myrtle & Spanish Moss, SC

Live Oak, Bluffton, SC

Mallards in flight, Summerton, South Carolina

Tri-Colored Heron, Story Island, SC

Black Skimmers take flight, Bull Island, South Carolina